Luther's Break With Rome

GUSTAV CARLBERG

LUTHER'S BREAK WITH ROME

WHY DID LUTHER BREAK WITH ROME?
AND WHY DO WE STAND ALOOF FROM THE
CHURCH OF ROME?

BY

GUSTAV CARLBERG, M.A., B.D.

PROFESSOR OF NEW TESTAMENT STUDIES AND
PEDAGOGY AT THE LUTHERAN THEOLOGICAL SEMINARY
SHEKOW, HUPEH, CHINA

WIPF & STOCK · Eugene, Oregon

Wipf and Stock Publishers
199 W 8th Ave, Suite 3
Eugene, OR 97401

Luther's Break With Rome
Why Did Luther Break With Rome?
And Why Do We Stand Aloof From The Church Of Rome?
By Carlberg, Gustav
Softcover ISBN-13: 978-1-7252-7502-7
Publication date 3/26/2020
Previously published by Lutheran Board of Publication, 1931

THIS BOOK IS

DEDICATED

TO

THE GREATER LUTHERAN CHURCH OF CHINA
FIRM FOUNDED ON THE
IMPREGNABLE ROCK OF SCRIPTURE TRUTH
AND UNITEDLY CONFESSING
THE HISTORIC ECUMENICAL CREEDS
AND THE AUGSBURG CONFESSION

FOREWORD

Divisions in the Church of Christ are a source of regret to sincere believers. Therefore they cannot but ask : Why have divisions come about? Why, and how long must they continue? Was the work of the Reformers wrong in aim and method and destructive in effect? Was Martin Luther a misguided and wicked man who sought the disruption and ruin of the Church? Was he a villain who would rend with ruthless hands the seamless robe of Christ, thus presuming to do what rough Romans hesitated to do after nailing Christ on the cross? Or, on the contrary, was the Reformation a movement wherein men guided and used by God sought thru constructive forces to restore that which error had already destroyed within the Church? And are those right after all who regard Martin Luther as the most truly heroic figure known to Church history since the days of the Apostle Paul?

Is it not true that the work of Luther and other reformers restored to the Church both the Word of God and the Sacraments as given to her in Apostolic times? And is it not also true that in so far as the principles of the Reformation have been received and adhered to in faith and practice there has resulted the restoration of the Church to the pristine purity and spiritual vitality of Apostolic times? Did not Luther after all, by God's grace, restore to the Church priceless treasures whereof she had been robbed? Furthermore, did he not justly urge the rejection by the Church of worthless tinsel and spurious gems foisted upon her by avaricious, selfish and blind leaders? And if this be the case, how could a restored and revitalized Church think of rejecting or abandoning the precious heritage so graciously given back to her?

This little unpretentious volume will, we think, give forceful, fair and clear answers to these and many similar questions. The reader will find it well worth while, by careful and thotful study, to possess himself of what the author has to offer.

As will be easily seen, the author has not written a book merely for the purpose of commemorating some important events that transpired some four hundred years ago, but rather does he aim to relate the reader to the throbbing life, stirring events, and vital facts of the great Restorative Movement of the sixteenth century in such a way as to elicit true ideal appreciation and practical appropriation of what God has given to His Church thru Luther and others who learned to know and to prize the great Gospel truth, "The just shall live by faith".

A. W. EDWINS, D D.

PERFATORY REMARKS

This book has grown out of the needs of the present situation on the mission field in China. To a Chinese Christian the divisions within the Church of Christ are more of a problem and a puzzle than they appear to a Western Christian with centuries of historic background, and viewpoints more or less consciously absorbed from his environment.

It is a common experience among missionaries to be requested to explain the difference between the Catholic and Protestant churches, or, as they put it, the difference between the Heaven Lord Doctrine and the Jesus or Gospel Doctrine.

For some years there has existed the need for a brief and concise statement regarding the fundamental differences between the Protestant and Catholic positions. In consequence of this need the Lutheran Board of Publication decided to have such a statement drawn up, and the choice fell on me to carry this decision into effect.

It was originally planned to publish this statement in the form of a tract, but on entering into the subject more deeply, it was found that a fuller treatment was merited and so the would-be tract was expanded into a small volume.

As the needs of Lutheran church members in China do not differ fundamentally from those elsewhere thruout the world, it was thot best to make the volume available also for church members in the West. Hence the book is being published simultaneously in both Chinese and English in the hopes that it will help to clarify and define the Lutheran position as over against the Roman Catholic and make us one and all more appreciative of our Lutheran heritage.

There never was a time when Lutheran Christians needed more to know just where they stand and to be willing to stand firm for what they believe than at the present.

Rome is engaging in an ever more intensive campaign for the furtherance of what one of her own writers has recently been pleased to term, "The New Imperialism of the Roman Catholic Church." This is nothing else but her new policy of peaceful penetration whereby she may attain to spiritual if not political dominance of the entire world. It is the old spirit in a more sophisticated garb.

Let us as Lutherans stand up for truth : Scriptural truth, Historical truth, Confessional truth. And let us not fear to come out into the open with what we have. Only error fears the light, but truth made manifest will dispel the miasmic vapors of error. The fearless champions of truth need have no misgivings regarding the final issue of their cause tho for a time they may be called upon to suffer for their convictions.

GUSTAV CARLBERG.

Shekow, Hupeh, China,
        April, 1931.

CONTENTS

CHAPTER I

PART I

CHAPTER II

The posting of the theses—Enemies
muster their forces—Theses directed against abuses in connection
with Indulgences—Origin of the
practice—Indulgences made to apply to souls in purgatory—A means
for gathering revenue—John Tetzel
and his preaching—Luther's tract,
Wider Hans Wurst—The ninety-
five theses not dogmatic statements—Typical theses.

CHAPTER III

Review of events of next three
years—Pope Leo takes action—
Luther summoned to appear before
Cajetan—His purpose to proceed
to Augsburg in spite of inner conflicts and misgivings—Takes his
stand on the Scriptures—Opponents help Luther to clarify his
views—Disputation with Eck at
Leipsic.

CHAPTER IV

Luther's vigorous polemic against
the papal system—Appeal to the
Christian Nobility of the German
Nation—Vindicates priesthood of
all believers—Exposes wordly pomp
of Pope and cardinals—Deals with
practical proposals for reform—
The Babylonian Captivity of the
Church—Refutes giving of communion in one element only—

CHAPTER IX

Sets forth main features of the
evangelical   position — Pivotal
truth, Justification by Faith—
Synopsis of first twenty-one articles
—Purpose of the Confession—
Reasons for omissions—Split in
Protestant ranks deplored—Lu-
therans take stand on Scripture—
Hopes for reconciliation with
Catholic party not realized—Lu-
theranism and Catholicism mutual-
ly incompatible.

PART II

CHAPTER X

Uncompromising attitude of Rome
—Hopes of reconciliation more re-
mote than ever—Council of Trent
—Liberal tendencies overruled—

Luther's Break With Rome

CHAPTER I

INTRODUCTION

The Roman Catholic Church is an ever present fact and an ever present problem to the Protestant Christian. We see their churches everywhere about us. In some cases there is a measure of cooperation with them, but mostly there is aloofness, and in a few instances there is open hostility and strife.

There are many things we hold in common. We profess a belief in the same God and in His Son, Jesus Christ. We are rooted in the same historic facts of the Apostolic Age and early Christianity. We possess the same Bible and we profess the same Apostles' Creed, and at the end of earth's pilgrimage we hope to attain to the same heaven of glory.

Yet there are important differences, important enough to have caused a rift in the church that has lasted now four hundred years and gives indications of continuing indefinitely.

It is the purpose of this treatise to examine in some detail the causes that brot about the breach in the church, and that continue to operate in keeping the two great branches of Christendom apart. It will be necessary, therefore, to pay especial attention to the events that led up to the break with the Roman hierarchy on the part of Luther and his followers, as well as to trace subsequent developments showing the relationship and attitude of the Church of Rome towards the Church of the Reformation.

It will also be necessary to take note of the differences in doctrine and practice that exist between the Roman Catholic Church and the Lutheran Church in particular.

This is not a polemic against the Roman Catholic Church. Tho it will be found necessary at times to speak with the utmost frankness and unreserve, this is done in love and in the sole interest of truth. We can freely admit that the Roman Catholic Church possesses many strong and excellent points and that there are hosts of sincere Christians among its membership whom we should be glad to recognize as fellow members of the body of Christ. At the same time we cannot close our eyes to the many glaring faults of the Roman Catholic system and in the interest of truth these must be dealt with.

However, the Roman Catholic Church does not have a monopoly on error, nor does the Lutheran Church have a monopoly on truth. Therefore I should be as ready to denounce error within the Lutheran Communion as I should be to acknowledge truth within the Catholic Communion.

Popery, ecclesiastical mummery, and intellectual obscurantism are unfortunately not dead within the Church of Christ and are likely to be met with in any communion, but we are persuaded that these things appear in a more glaring and aggravated form in the Church of Rome than anywhere else. By having these errors pointed out to us thru the forceful object lesson of the Roman Catholic Church we shall better be able to recognize these faults within our own church and take measures to combat and eradicate them. The

Reformation of the sixteenth century to become truly significant and operative in the church life of the twentieth century must become a repetitive process so that the church continues to reform herself, continues to return again and again to Christ the source and well-spring of her life and existence. This can be done only thru a full reliance on the help of the Holy Spirit and thru a proper use of the inspired teachings of the Holy Scriptures. In this way the church will be renewed and made into a fit instrument of God for the doing of His will and work in the world.

PART I

Why Did Luther Break With Rome?

For, behold, Jehovah commandeth, and He will smite the great house with breaches, and the little house with clefts.

(AMOS 6: 11)

Part I

Why Did Luther Break With Rome?

CHAPTER II

The Ninety-five Theses: A Fearless Challenge.

The posting by Luther of his ninety-five theses on the church door of Wittenberg on the eve of All Saints' Day, October 31, 1517, is the world-famous event commonly regarded as the beginning of the Protestant Reformation.

Luther had already during two years previous to this been busy, in writing and preaching, pointing out the abuses within the church, but up to this time no event had so stirred the imagination and received so much publicity as this fearless challenge on the part of the Wittenberg professor to anyone who wished to meet with him and discuss the subject of indulgences both as to their status and the abuses which had crept in in connection with their use.

But if the posting of the ninety-five theses was a signal for the friends of Luther to rally around his banner, it was likewise a signal for his enemies to muster their forces of opposition in an effort to muzzle forever the mouth of one who had dared to raise his voice in criticism of the church and its doings.

Luther was denounced as a heretic and proceedings were at once instituted against him which were eventually to issue in his outlawry and excommunication. But let us note carefully here that Luther's "sin" against the church consisted chiefly in pointing out abuses in connection with the sale of indulgences, abuses which were later to be admitted by Rome and partly eradicated.

Luther's ninety-five theses were not directed against Indulgences as an institution in their original intent as offering remission of temporal penances. His attack was against the flagrant abuses that had grown up around the sale of indulgences so as to cover remission for present, past, and future sins of one's own, as well as apply to the remission of penalties for the departed languishing souls in purgatory.

It is well to stop briefly here and examine into the origin of the practice of granting indulgences and the growth of the abuses in connection with their sale.

The theory underlying the granting of indulgences was founded on the doctrine of the superabundant merits of Christ, Mary, and all the saints. This treasury of the church, as it was called, had been committed to the jurisdiction of the Pope, who as successor of Peter was the keeper of the keys of heaven, and could draw on this inexhaustible deposit of merit for the use of such as were lacking in merit of their own.

The doctrine was fully elaborated by Thomas Aquinas in the thirteenth century, but the actual practice of granting indulgences originated at a much earlier date. As far back as 877 Pope John VIII granted what became known as the Crusading Indulgence to soldiers who enlisted in the wars against the Moslems, promising liberation from certain acts of penance and the corresponding punishments in purgatory.

These indulgences were later extended to apply also to such as were willing to furnish money for the equipping of a substitute, and hence became an important means not only for the recruiting of soldiers, but for gathering of funds for the army and for other purposes.[1]

On August 3, 1476, Pope Sixtus IV issued a bull making the force of indulgences apply to the souls in purgatory.[2] Tho this dogma was not officially sanctioned by the church the practice of granting indulgences for the dead became very widespread and offered a valuable means for increasing the revenue of the church.[3]

In Luther's time by far the most famous, or rather infamous, vendor of indulgences was John Tetzel who had been made head of one of the Indulgence Commissions in Germany. These indulgences had been promulgated by Pope Leo X ostensibly for the purpose of securing funds for the building of St. Peter's Church at Rome, but in reality they were intended to help replenish a depleted treasury. By special arrangements with the Archbishop of Magdeburg the Pope was to receive half of the proceeds while the Archbishop, Albert of Mainz, was to retain the other half to be used in the extension of his ecclesiastical domains.[4]

Tetzel's specialty was the offering of indulgences for the souls in purgatory. One of his sermons preached at this time contains the following impassioned plea : "Do you not hear your parents and other deceased wailing and crying, 'have pity on us, have pity on us', we are suffering the most grievous punishment and torture from which you are able to set us free by the payment of a trifling alms ?"[5]

In a tract written by Luther in 1541 entitled Wider Hans Wurst he explains in some detail the preaching of indulgences as carried on by John Tetzel which moved Luther to issue his ninety-five theses in protest. According to Luther, Tetzel maintained among other things that the red Indulgence Cross he carried was just as efficacious towards the forgiveness of sins as the cross of Christ; that if St. Peter were here now he would not possess greater grace and power than Tetzel had. Indeed, he would not exchange places with Peter in heaven since he had redeemed more souls by his indulgences than had St. Peter by his preaching. He also claimed that when money was placed in the coffer for a soul in purgatory such a soul would immediately enter heaven when the money clinked against the bottom of the chest. Luther also maintained Tetzel offered indulgences for future sins. Tho this has been denied by Catholic writers, the common people of that day certainly were under that impression as Luther had ample opportunity of learning from the confessional, from which source he gained much of his information regarding the evil results of the indulgence traffic.[6]

Luther's ninety-five theses were not meant to be dogmatic statements presenting his views on indulgences, but were intended to point to some of the manifest abuses in connection with their use, and to serve as a basis for discussion with a view to arousing the church to action.[7] A few of the typical theses are given to show their general tenor.

1. "When our Lord and Master Jesus Christ says: 'Repent ye,' etc., He wishes the

entire life of the Christian to be one of true repentance."

5. "The Pope neither will nor can remit other punishments than those he himself or the decrees of the Church have imposed".

8. "Penances are to be imposed only on the living and no such obligations should be imposed on the dying."

36. "Every Christian who exhibits true contrition has a right to full remission of punishment and guilt even without letters of indulgence."

38. "The remission granted by the Pope is however by no means to be despised since it is a declaration of the Divine pardon."

43. "Christians should be taught that one who gives to the poor or lends to the needy does better than if he purchases indulgence."

81. "This indiscriminate preaching of indulgence makes it difficult for even learned men to safeguard the reverence due to the Pope against the calumnies or keen questionings of the laity."

82. "As for instance: 'Why does not the Pope empty purgatory from most holy love and the supreme necessity of the souls, the most justifiable of all reasons, since he has redeemed countless souls for filthy lucre towards the erection of a church, the most trivial reason of any?'"

92. "Away, therefore, with all those prophets who say to the people of Christ: 'Peace, peace', and there is no peace."

93. "Godspeed to all those prophets who say to the people of Christ: 'The Cross, the Cross,' and there is no cross."

94. "Christians should be admonished to strive to follow Christ their head thru suffering, death, and hell;

95. "And thus trust to enter heaven 'thru many tribulations', rather than depend on the security of a false peace."[8]

In considering Luther's attack on indulgences in his ninety-five theses and elsewhere, the following three points should be carefully noted:

1) Luther was not attacking a formal dogma of the church, but a practice

which had become widespread within the church.

2) Luther did not propose to do away with indulgences, but merely restrict their use to remission of canonical penance.

3) He desired to direct attention towards the misunderstandings and abuses that had become prevalent in connection with indulgences with a view to having these errors eradicated.

In spite of Luther's earnest representations as to the real nature and intent of his theses, his opponents persisted in regarding them as dogmatic staten.ents, and immediately instituted heresy proceedings which lasted three years and finally led to Luther's conviction on the charge of heresy and his outlawry by the church and empire.

CHAPTER III

Heresy Proceedings: Rome's Reply to Luther's Challenge.

Let us review briefly the significant events of the next three years, culminating in the famous Diet of Worms where Luther was tried and convicted of heresy and his writings consigned to the fire.

Pope Leo was at first not disposed to take Luther seriously. On receiving a copy of Luther's theses he is reported to have said : "A drunken German has written this stuff; he will think differently when he is sober." But Luther's opponents would not let the matter rest. The leaders among the Dominicans, a rival order of the Augustinians, to which Luther belonged, sent a list of charges to Rome accusing the Wittenberg professor of a number of heresies, chiefly that he had in previous writings attacked the prevailing theology of the church and appealed from the schoolmen to the authority of the Bible on such questions as sin and grace, good works,

justification by faith, and free will, besides
his criticism of indulgences.[10]

The Pope now felt constrained to take
action. Luther was forthwith summoned to
Rome to appear in person to answer to the
charges brot against him. On representations of the University of Wittenberg and
Elector Fredrick, who had already shown
himself friendly towards Luther's cause,
Luther was spared the journey to Rome, and
the Pope charged his legate, Cajetan, to
examine Luther at the Diet of Augsburg in
1518.[11]

Luther went to Augsburg fully persuaded in his own mind that he went to the stake
and that he would be burned as a heretic
before another three months were gone. His
friends along the way warned him and tried
to dissuade him from his purpose, saying,
they would surely burn him at Augsburg.

Luther, however, was firm in his purpose
to proceed in spite of inner conflicts and
misgivings. Like Paul on his way to
Jerusalem, he was ready both to be bound and
to suffer, if need be for the name of Christ.
"Let the Lord's will be done", he wrote to a

friend. "Even at Augsburg, yea, in the midst of His enemies, Jesus Christ rules. Let Christ live, let Martin die and every sinner, as it is written. God will be exalted to my salvation. It is needful that we be rejected either by men or by God. God is true tho every man be a liar".

At Augsburg every pressure was brot to bear on Luther to force him to yield from his position, but Luther took his stand firmly on the Scriptures and for the unalienable right of the individual to liberty in thot and conscience, as over against unquestioned submission to ecclesiastical authority.[12]

Luther's opponents unwittingly did him a good turn in that they forced him to clarify his views and bring his convictions to their logical conclusion in opposition to the Roman system. In one of his pamphlets he thanks his opponents for promoting his theological training and helping him to get to the bottom of things.

One of his most zealous and outstanding opponents was his one time friend John Eck, who challenged Luther to a series of disputations on the questions at issue. These disputations were held at Leipsic in June and July of 1519, covering a period of two weeks or more, and dealt with such questions as the primacy of the Pope, repentance, indulgences, purgatory, etc. Both sides claimed the victory. For Luther the importance of these disputations, which he regarded as quite useless and a waste of time, was that they mark a definite step in his emancipation from the papal system. Here for the first time he denied the divine right and origin of the papacy, and the infallibility of a general church council. From now on he must take his stand on the Scriptures alone.[13]

CHAPTER IV

Luther's Campaign Literature: Three Great Writings of the Reformation Period.

After the Leipsic disputations Luther saw the hopelessness of looking for reform from the Roman Church and enters on a period of vigorous polemic against the papal system. He publishes three important writings at this time in rapid succession. In July of 1520 he sent forth his stirring appeal, To the Christian Nobility of the German Nation.

Before a month was gone no less than 4000 copies had been published and a new edition was called for. In this book, which has been characterized as Luther's declaration of war against the papacy, he makes his appeal to the Christian laity to rise up, not with force of arms, but with united effort by legal means with the help of God to bring about needed reform within the church.

The book, written in forceful German and impassioned style, struck a responsive chord in the hearts of the German people. There are three parts of which the first vindicates the fundamental principle of the priesthood of all believers as over against the priestcraft of the Roman system. The difference between clergy and laity is one of function not of estate.

The second part of the book is directed against the worldly pomp and ostentation on the part of the popes and cardinals; and in the third part he sets forth various practical proposals for needed reform. Here he deals with such questions as celibacy of the clergy, homage paid to the Pope, his temporal power, masses for the dead, processions and festivals, monasteries and monastic vows, fasts, begging, needed reform in the universities, etc. The national vices of drinking, usury, and extravagance in dress, are strongly condemned.

In concluding this stirring appeal to the German people, Luther says: "My greatest care and fear is lest my cause be not condemned by men; by which I should know for certain that it does not please God. Therefore let them freely go to work, Pope, bishop, priest, monk, or doctor; they are the true people to persecute the truth, as they have always done. May God grant us all a Christian understanding, and especially to the Christian nobility of the German nation true spiritual courage, to do what is best for our unhappy church."[14]

The Babylonian Captivity of the Church was published in October of 1520 in Latin as it was intended for the scholars. In this work, regarded by many as his most important, Luther attacks the sacramental system of the church. First, he refutes from Scripture the practice of giving the communion in one element only to the laity, citing the words of Christ, "Drink ye *all* of this". He concludes that the church has no more right to take away the cup from the laity than the bread, and characterizes this practice as an act of impiety and tyranny.

In the second place he refutes the doctrine of transubstantiation, denying the miraculous change of the substance of the elements, but maintaining the real presence of the body and the blood in the sacrament.

Thirdly, he attacks the sacrifice of the mass on the ground that the Eucharist is a gift from God to man, not a gift from man to God whereby he may acquire merit. This

he characterizes as the most impious bondage
of all since it has brot in its train a host of
other abuses. He makes a plea for the return
to the simplicity of the original institution
of the Lord's Supper as a thankful commemoration of the atoning death of Christ, with a
blessing attached to it, namely the forgiveness of sins to those who receive the sacrament
in faith.[15]

Luther's third campaign writing is
entitled, Christian Freedom. This little
booklet, which has been termed a pearl among
Luther's writings, presents the following two
apparently contradictory theses: A Christian
is free and not subject to anyone; A Christian
is in all things a servant and a slave and
subject to everyone. The former is secured
thru faith alone aside from works, but when
once gained the second holds true, he is in
duty bound to serve his fellow man with all
his power. This by virtue of love. Good
works do not make a man good, but a good
man will perform good works. Faith binds
the Christian to God, love binds him to his
fellowman. In the words of Paul: "Tho I
am free from all men, I brot myself under
bondage to all, that I might gain more."
(I Cor. 9 : 19).[16]

CHAPTER V

Luther and the Pope: Letters and Bulls.

On instigation of Carl von Miltiz, the Pope's chamberlain, Luther sent a letter to Pope Leo X in which he commiserates him on his unenviable position as the tool of self-seeking politicians, and deprecates the corruption of those in power in the church. He holds fast his right to interpret Scripture and his Christian freedom, and hopes the church will institute the needed reforms which would do away with the abuses patent to everyone.

He begs the Pope not to believe people who would elevate him above every other human and give to him alone the power to interpret Scripture. He encloses his pamphlet on Christian Freedom so the Pope may know what his views are.[17]

Luther's gradual change of attitude towards the Pope is clearly seen from his three letters to the Pope written in 1518, 1519, and 1520, respectively. In the first letter he addresses the Pope as an obedient son of the vicar of Christ; in his second letter

47

he still addresses him as a humble subject, yet refusing firmly to part with his own conscientious convictions. In his third and last letter, the gist of which is given above, he addresses the Pope as an equal with great respect for his personal character yet denouncing the sins of the Roman see in the most unsparing terms. Here is a sample of the language used:

> "The Church of Rome, formerly the most holy of all the churches, has become the most lawless den of thieves, the most shameless of all brothels, the very kingdom of sin, death, and hell; so that not even antichrist, if he were to come, could devise any addition to its wickedness."

> "Meanwhile you Leo are sitting like a lamb in the midst of wolves, like Daniel in the midst of lions, and, with Ezekiel you dwell among scorpions. What opposition can you alone make to these monstrous evils?"[18]

It is difficult to know just what purpose Luther had in mind in penning these missives to the Pope. Certain it is that they did not cause the Pope to feel any more kindly disposed towards Luther, nor did he abate from his firm purpose to bring the recalcitrant Wittenberg Professor to speedy terms.

Even while Luther was penning his third and last letter to the Pope and before he had sent it on its way, the 'Bull of Excommunication had already arrived. Nearly three years had now passed since the posting of the world-famous ninety-five theses. The Bull was the Pope's reply to Luther's theses and not only condemns him as an arch heretic, but with him the whole reformatory movement.[19]

The Bull, dated June 16, 1520, is of the greatest importance historically as marking the definite break between the Roman Church and the new movement for reform. It condemns Luther and his followers in unsparing terms and would consign him and his writings to the fire, in answer to which Luther kindles a fire outside the gate of Wittenberg and with solemn ceremony consigns the Bull of the Pope to the flames with the words adapted from Joshua's indictment of Achan the thief : "Because thou hast troubled the saints of the Lord, let eternal fire consume thee". By this act Luther has burnt his bridges behind him and the breach with Rome is made permanent and complete.[20]

The Bull is known by the name Exurge Domine from the opening invocation from the Psalmist: "Arise O God, plead thine own cause!" (Ps. 74:22). After invoking God, St. Peter, St. Paul, and all the saints against the enemies of the church the Pope enumerates in forty-one consecutive articles the heresies of Luther in matters pertaining to original sin, concupiscence, the sacrament of penance, justification by faith, communion in both kinds, the treasury of the church, indulgences, excommunication, the papal power, authority of general councils, the unjust condemnation of Hus, the burning of heretics, war against the Turks, freewill, purgatory, the destruction of the mendicant orders, and others. The Bull threatens to put Luther and his followers under the ban unless he retracts within sixty days, and ends with provisions for its promulgation and execution, threatening dire punishment to those who dare disobey its mandates.[21]

The fate of the Bull at Luther's hands has already been indicated, and after the expiration of the time of grace allotted, the Bull was followed in due course by a Bull of Excommunication on January 3, 1521, which was put into immediate effect by Emperor Charles V in the Netherlands, but not in Germany out of regard for Elector Fredrick, Luther's own prince, who insisted that Luther should not be condemned unheard, in consequence of which he was summoned to appear before the Diet at Worms to answer in person to the charges brot against him.

CHAPTER VI

Luther at Worms: A Courageous Stand.

Luther regarded the summons to Worms as a call from God and as an opportunity to witness to the truth.   He would not be dissuaded from his purpose to go there either by friend or foe.   Someone reminded him of the fate of Hus who had been burnt at the stake one hundred years previously regardless of safe conduct.   Luther declared that, "if they would make a fire that would fill the sky between Wittenberg and Worms, he would go on in the name of the Lord, since they had summoned him, and would walk into the jaws of Behemoth and confess Christ between his teeth."   He reminded his friends that tho Hus was burnt, the truth was not burnt, and Christ still lives.

"You may expect everything from me except fear or recantation", he wrote to his friend, Spalatin, "I shall not flee, still less recant."

When plans were set afoot by his opponents to swerve him from his purpose he declared he would enter Worms even if there were as many devils in it as there were tiles on the roofs of the houses.

His journey to Worms in an open wagon accompanied by some friends from Wittenberg and preceded by the imperial herald resembled a march of triumph. People everywhere came out in great numbers to see the man who had dared singlehanded to defy the power of Rome.

At several places along the way he preached to large audiences maintaining his stand for the pure Gospel of Jesus Christ as over against the work-righteousness and the traditions of the church.

Luther arrived at Worms on the morning of April 16, 1521 amid a great concourse of people. He was dressed in his monastic gown, and his first words on alighting from the carriage were: "God will be with me".

The next day in the afternoon he was conducted to the hall of the diet where he faced an august assembly of papal legates, archbishops, dukes, margraves, princes.

counts, deputies of the imperial cities, ambassadors of foreign courts and other dignitaries, with the youthful monarch Charles V in the midst.

When confronted with the question whether he would be prepared to recant any part of his writings, a generous pile of which were lying on the table, he asked that their titles might be read. According to prearrangement with his advisers Luther then asked for time to reflect. "Since it is a question of faith and the salvation of souls, and concerns the Word of God, than which nothing is greater in heaven or earth, and which it behooves us all to revere, it would be rash for me to proffer anything without due reflection."

Luther's request was granted and he was given a day's respite which he spent in prayer and conference with his friends.

On the afternoon of the 18th Luther appeared for the final hearing. Being asked whether after due reflection he was still prepared to defend all his writings, he pointed out that his writings were not all of one class and it would be unjust to condemn them all alike, and that since he was liable to err he wanted to be shown from the Scriptures where he was in the wrong, and if thus convinced he would most readily revoke and be the first to throw his books into the fire.

Luther distinguished three classes of his writings :

1) Evangelical writings, dealing with practical religion and morals. Even his enemies would have to admit that these were without reproach and worthy to be read by all Christians.

2) Polemical writings against the Pope and the papists and their doings. If he should revoke these he would but be strengthening the tyranny which was devastating Christendom.

3) Polemical writings against individuals who have upheld the power of the Pope. In the case of these he admits he may have gone too far, but he will nevertheless not recant anything for fear it would give comfort to his enemies and work harm to the cause for which he stood.

The emperor's spokesman reproved Luther for seeking to evade the issue and demanded a direct answer, "without horns", to the question whether he will revoke and recant the errors contained in his works. Luther replied that he would give an answer without "horns or teeth", that is, without ambiguity or intentional offence. He then gave his answer which has gone down the annals of time as one of the great sayings of history :

> "Unless I am convinced by the testimony of the Holy Scriptures or by clear arguments, since I do not believe the Pope or the Councils alone, as it is evident that they have erred and contradicted one another, I am held fast by the Scriptures as adduced by me, and my conscience is bound by the Word of God; I neither can nor will retract anything, since it is neither safe nor right to act against conscience. God help me. Amen."

Luther's courageous stand elicited the admiration of many members of the diet who were not counted among his adherents, but his own prince, Elector Fredrick, was enthusiastic in his approval. Luther was conducted to his lodgings by his friends, and on arriving there threw up his hands in joyful exclamation : "I am thru, I am thru". He declared to Spalatin and others that if he had a thousand heads he would "rather have them all cut off one by one than make one recantation."[22]

On May 26, 1521, the Emperor signed the edict outlawing Luther, and on the following day his books were burnt. On the way back from Worms, Luther was carried off to the castle Wartburg thru the contrivance of Elector Fredrick.

Here in this quiet retreat amid pleasant surroundings he passed several months as the honored guest of the Elector. Assuming the disguise of a country gentleman and the name, Squire George, his identity was not known except by his closest attendants. In writing to his friends he would humorously style his place of retreat as the "Mountain Top", or the "Isle of Patmos", etc. By means of a lively correspondence he kept in touch with the outside world and continued to direct the great movement of which he was the recognized head.

With unflagging zeal and energy he devoted himself to the translation of the Scriptures into the German language. As to the Old Testament he found it a great and laborious task to "force the Hebrew writers to speak German". He succeeded remarkably well, nevertheless, and his translation of the Bible became one of the most influential means of fixing and standardizing the German language. Such was his industry and application that in less than three months he had finished a rough draft of the New Testament, which was published in 1522.[23]

CHAPTER VII

The Secret of Luther's Courage: His Governing Principles.

Let us leave Luther busy at work in his mountain retreat and return once more to our question, Why did Luther break with Rome? How could he take the stand he did at Worms against Pope, Roman Curia, Emperor and staff, in the face of certain excommunication and almost as certain death? Why did he not retract? Mainly for two reasons.

The first reason is to be found in Luther's soul experience. The way in which he had found peace with God was not the way prescribed by the church. Fastings, ascetic practices, good works, prayers to and the good offices of the saints, masses, sacraments, and all the other paraphernalia of priestcraft were powerless to bring release to his sin-burdened conscience. But when he saw as by revelation: "The just shall live by faith", a new wonderful peace flooded his soul.

This soul experience of Luther has rightly been termed the most significant fact of the entire reformation movement, a fact which could not be gainsaid nor controverted by the arguments of opponents nor altered or eradicated by papal bulls or threats.

The second reason why Luther could not retract is to be found in his attitude towards the Word of God. He took his stand on the impregnable rock of Scripture truth, and from this position all the assaults of the enemy were unable to dislodge him.

The Scriptures, and the God who spoke thru the Scriptures, was the true source of all authority in matters of doctrine and morals, not the dogmas and traditions of the church. Not the decrees of popes nor the decisions of church councils, but the God of the Scriptures, speaking thru them to the Spirit enlightened conscience of the believer, was the true seat of authority. From this position Luther would not suffer himself to be removed.

Out of Luther's soul experience in seeking and finding God, and out of his conception of the Scriptures as the seat of ultimate authority in spiritual things, grew the two fundamental principles of the Reformation :

1) Justification by faith alone, and,
2) The Bible as the only rule of faith and practice.

These two great truths, rediscovered and reemphasized by Luther, were not only the mainsprings of his own actions, but are the potent principles underlying all movements towards the liberation of the human mind and spirit during the centuries that have followed since his day.

We have already seen that separation from the Roman Catholic Church was not a part of Luther's original plan. He was forced into this position by the uncompromising attitude and the persistent agitation against him on the part of his opponents. Luther had in mind a purification of the church and the eradication of the abuses and false doctrines that had grown up and had all but smothered the spiritual life of the church.

Luther contemplated bringing about the needed reforms in the church in a peaceable manner. His attitude towards the employment of forcible means towards attaining his purpose is clearly shown by the part he played in restraining the hotheads and radicals at Wittenberg who during his absence at Wartburg began to instigate riots and disturbances in the churches with a view to changing the old order of things. Luther hastened to Wittenberg at no small risk to himself and with a firm hand put down the disturbances and with words of strong rebuke managed to cool the ardor of his too enthusiastic followers.

The principles governing his attitude and efforts towards reform may be summed up as follows:

1) There should be no forcible subversion of the present order.

2) Rebellion is never justified, no matter how just the cause.

3) Revolutionary measures belong alone to the Christian governments, not to the people.

4) A Christian can speak, preach, write, and thus practice the Gospel and assist in its spread. Also he can by exhortation and counsel induce governments to take action.[24]

CHAPTER VIII

The Diet of Augsburg: The Birth of a Notable Document.

For some years the evangelical movement grew more or less unhampered, but in 1529 at the Diet of Spires, Roman Catholic representatives were in the majority and took measures intended to put an end to the reformatory movement. Here the evangelical delegates presented a formal protest from which originated the name Protestants as a common designation for all those who adhered to the principles of reform as advocated by Luther and his followers.[25]

In 1530 the Emperor summoned a diet to meet at Augsburg with the purpose of inducing the Protestants to return to the old faith and thus restore the long lost harmony within the church. He also desired to take measures to stem the threatened invasion by the Turks who had already advanced into Austria and were now laying siege to Vienna.

Charles had just succeeded in crushing the rebellion in Spain; he had conquered France, and composed the differences between himself and the Pope, forcing this dignitary to crown him Emperor of the Holy Roman Empire. The crowning took place at Barcelona in 1529. Yet two great tasks remained to be accomplished before he could hope to look for tranquility within his huge realm which included the greater part of Europe and the Spanish possessions in the New World.

The Turk must be vanquished and for this he needed the support of the powerful German princes. The troubles within the church must be settled as a divided church meant a divided empire and would lead inevitably to religious wars in the future. The latter was by far the greatest and most difficult problem and was to prove the rock on which his own ship of state would founder and meet disaster bringing his own political fortunes to an inglorious end.[26]

The Protestant princes and the theologians whom they had invited as counsellors came to Augsburg with high hopes of being able to present their cause in such a manner as to remove the most serious obstacles to a continued unity within the church. These hopes were not to be realized due to the uncompromising attitude of the Catholic party.

At the instigation of the Dukes of Bavaria, Dr. Eck of the Ingolstadt theological faculty had prepared a series of 404 articles from the Lutheran writings which he attacked in most unsparing terms, denouncing Luther and his followers as heretics and disturbers of the peace of the church.

It became clear to the defenders of the evangelical viewpoint that they must present a clear statement of the articles of faith for which they stood and not only as originally intended present a list of the abuses in the church for which they sought a remedy.[27]

Thus was born the Augsburg Confession, a document that deserves to take its place in history alongside of the ancient creeds of Christendom and which may be justly regarded as the charter of freedom from which all movements for civil and religious liberty of modern times have sprung.

Since Luther had to be left at Coburg due to a lack of safe conduct it fell to the lot of Luther's trusted colleague Melanchthon to be the chief sponsor for bringing the Confession into being. Tho based on three other documents previously prepared partly by Luther and partly by Melanchthon, the Confession is nevertheless in its final form and arrangement the work of Melanchthon who worked unceasingly up to the very last moment getting it into proper shape for presentation at the Diet.[28]

Melanchthon himself relates how the confession was prepared. It was discussed by the princes and theologians and when completed was sent to Luther for approval. Luther signified his assent and felt that a great step forward had been taken saying he was glad "to have lived to this hour in which Christ has been preached publicly by his illustrious confessors in such a large assembly in such a very beautiful confession". He also confessed that he himself would not have been able to "tread so softly and gently" as brother Melanchthon had done.[29]

The Confession was signed by seven princes and representatives of two independent cities and was read before the Emperor, the princes, papal representatives, and the ecclesiastical dignitaries on June 25, 1530, in the chapel of the episcopal palace where the Emperor had his lodgings.[30]

The day of the public reading of the Augsburg Confession has gone down in history as one of the great days of Lutheranism along with October 31, 1517, and the date of Luther's famous stand at Worms, April 18, 1521.

Four hundred years after the presentation of the Augsburg Confession on June 25, 1930, there was held in the city of Augsburg a great celebration in commemoration of the event, in which Lutheran and Reformed representatives from all over the world participated.

Well may the church celebrate an event that gave birth to a document that has proved the rallying point of the various branches of the Lutheran church thruout four centuries, and which forms the basis for every important confessional document in the entire Protestant church.

CHAPTER IX

The Augsburg Confession: A Testimony to Scripture Truth.

The Augsburg Confession presents in plain simple and lucid language the chief articles of faith of the Lutheran Church and defines her position in clear and unmistakable terms as over against those who would obscure or falsify the plain teachings of Scripture.

There are twenty-one articles on doctrine setting forth the main features of the evangelical position, and seven articles against abuses such as withholding the cup from the laity, celibacy of the clergy, the mass, confession, monastic vows, and secular power of the clergy.

The central and pivotal truth of the Confession as well as its organizing principle is set forth in the fourth article, Justification by Faith.

The first three articles lay the foundation for the fourth in treating respectively of the Unity of the Divine Essence, The Nature and

Universality of Sin, and The Person and Work of Christ.

After article four follows logically article five on how faith is obtained thru the instrumentality of the Word and Sacraments, and article six speaks of its results in good works as commanded by God.

Article seven deals with the nature and unity of the church, and article eight asserts the effectiveness of the means of grace irrespective of the nature of those who dispense them.

Articles nine and ten deal with the sacraments. Then follow in succession articles dealing with confession, repentance, necessity of faith in connection with the use of the sacraments, ecclesiastical order, rites and usages in the church, attitude of believers towards civil affairs, final judgment, freedom of the will, cause of sin, good works, and worship of the saints.

The conclusion to the first part states: "This is about the sum of our doctrine, in which it can be seen there is nothing that varies from the Scriptures or from the Church Catholic, or from the Church of Rome as

known from its writers. This being the case
they judge harshly who insist that our
teachers be regarded as heretics. The disagreement, however, is on certain abuses
which have crept into the church without
rightful authority.'' Here follows a plea for
clemency with the evangelical churches in not
following the same rites as the Church of
Rome.[31]

The purpose of the Augsburg Confession
gives us a clue to its form and content. It
was meant to be a statement of the irreducible
minimum of the articles of faith held by the
evangelicals which they could not relinquish
and still remain true to their conscience. It
was couched in mild and inoffensive language
so as to further the object of reconciliation
between the two parties. It was never meant
to be a complete statement of all the articles
of faith held by the evangelicals, but a
refutation of the slanderous reports that had
been circulated by their opponents, and a
proof that nothing subversive of the true
doctrines of the church was taught by them.

Thus it comes about that the Confession
is silent on several of the cardinal doctrines of

faith such as, the supreme authority of the Scriptures in matters of faith and morals, the universal priesthood of believers, the nature and office of the Holy Spirit, the doctrine of the invisible church as contrasted with the ecclesiastical organization. Such matters as the papal authority, purgatory, the spurious sacraments, etc., are passed over in silence.

Thus while the Confession can be truly said to present the essence and spirit of the evangelical teaching, it can by no means be said to include all that was taught and believed in the evangelical churches.

The omissions from the Confession are easily understandable from the earnest desire on the part of the evangelicals to go to the limit in the direction of conciliation with the other party without sacrifice of essential principles.[32]

It has been greatly deplored by writers in Reformed circles that the Lutherans at Augsburg did not show a conciliatory spirit towards the Zwinglians as well as towards the Catholics, so that Protestantism at this time might be able to present a united front and receive a better hearing before their common opponents.[33]

None deplore the split in the Protestant ranks any more than the Lutherans, but the fact remains that nothing hindered the Zwinglian representatives from signing the Augsburg Confession and making it their own had they been willing to do so. In fact their opposition was due to one point alone as on all other points they had already at the conference at Marburg in 1529 signified their substantial agreement.

This one point of disagreement related to the fundamental doctrine of the Lord's Supper, and here they chose to take their stand not on the revealed word of Scripture as did the Lutherans, but on their own interpretation of that Word. Where the Lutherans took their refuge in the words of Christ, "this is my body", and, "this is my blood", the Zwinglians insisted on their own interpretation of the words of Christ for which they could show no Scripture warrant.

In this matter then the Lutheran theologians and representatives were consistently following out their fundamental principle of letting Scripture be the sole arbiter in matters pertaining to both doctrine and morals, and in this respect they presented a determined front towards their foes as well as their friends.

Article ten of the Confession sets forth this doctrine briefly and clearly thus :

> "Of the Lord's Supper, they teach, that the Body and Blood of Christ are truly present, and are distributed to those who eat in the Supper of the Lord; and they disapprove of those who teach otherwise."

After carefully and prayerfully considering such Scripture passages as Matt. 26: 26-28, and parallel passages; I Cor. 10: 16; 11 : 23-30; which admittedly are the only passages in the Bible that deal directly with the Lord's Supper, could anyone conscientiously refuse to put his stamp of approval on Article Ten of the Augsburg Confession ?

The Diet of Augsburg came to a close with the two parties of the church further apart than at the beginning of the Diet. The hopes and efforts of the Lutheran representatives for a reconciliation had come to naught.

They were gradually made to realize that the Emperor and the representatives of the Roman Catholic Church had come to Augsburg, not for the purpose of making concessions to the Lutherans, but to persuade them by peaceful means if possible to recede from their position, failing this they were prepared to use force in bringing them back into the fold of the church.

For this reason the Catholic representatives did not present a confession of their own as a basis for comparison and negotiation, but they offered a confutation of the Lutheran confession, which tho moderate in terms, nevertheless does not yield any of the essential points at issue.

The Diet of Augsburg marks a definite crisis in the reformation movement as it demonstrated beyond a doubt the futility of expecting agreement on matters of doctrine and practice. Lutheranism and Romanism in their fundamental concepts and outlook are shown to be mutually incompatible. They cannot carry on side by side in the same organization.

"Lutheranism is based on the Word of God. Catholicism is based on the authority of the church. Lutheranism holds that the institutions of men have no dominion over the conscience. Catholicism holds that the institutions of the church bind the conscience as conditions of salvation. Lutheranism teaches that the Confession itself is open to revision and to improvement in statement. Catholicism pronounces anathema on all who reject her canons and decrees."[34]

PART II

Why Do We Stand Aloof From The Church Of Rome?

Be thou watchful and establish the things that remain, which were ready to die, for I have found no works of thine perfected before my God.

Remember therefore how thou hast received and didst hear; and KEEP it and REPENT. (Rev. 3 : 2,3)

Part II

Why Do We Stand Aloof From The Church Of Rome?

CHAPTER X

Later Developments: Rome Recedes Further from Us.

We have traced in some detail in the foregoing the causes and events that led up to Luther's break with Rome. We have followed the movement for reform within the church from the eventful posting of the ninety-five theses by Luther in 1517 to the no less eventful day at Augsburg in 1530 which saw the birth of the Augsburg Confession marking the permanent establishment of the Lutheran Communion as a body of believers independent of and distinct from the Roman Catholic Church.

Let us now address ourselves to the question, Why does the Lutheran Church, or we as Lutherans, continue to hold ourselves aloof from the Church of Rome?

We have already demonstrated that the underlying cause for Luther's break with the Roman hierarchy was the latter's uncompromising attitude towards the reformers and the unwillingness of the church to correct the abuses that were a source of grief and concern to every earnest and right thinking soul.

The uncompromising attitude of the Roman Church as manifested so clearly at Augsburg has continued up to the present time, and developments within the Catholic Church since that day have caused the rift between the two great bodies of the church to widen. This makes any effort at agreement and conciliation seem far more futile and far more remote than at any previous time. The Lutheran representatives at Augsburg went as far as conscience and the manifest teachings of the Word of God would permit them to go in the direction of conciliation; further than they went we dare not and cannot go.

One of the fruits of the Diet of Augsburg was the calling of a General Council of the Church with the purpose of discussing matters of doctrine and taking measures for the remedying of the most flagrant abuses. The Council, tho promised and planned for by the Emperor at an early date, was not called until December 13, 1545, two months before the death of Luther, the main champion of the Reformation Movement.

The Council of Trent, taking its name from the place of meeting in Northern Italy, was carried on intermittently for the space of eighteen years. The Council is of great significance in the history of the church as marking the final fixing of the doctrinal system of the Church of Rome as over against the Evangelicals, and the definite completion and standardization of the doctrinal basis of the Church of Rome for all time.[35]

Liberalizing tendencies were not wanting at the Council. Many of the ablest of the members were in favor of recognizing such evangelical principles as justification by faith alone, and the supreme authority of the Scriptures. But the Roman Curia by means of diplomacy and intrigue succeeded in overruling all the more liberal tendencies within the Council.

Some crying abuses were abolished, it is true, which had a wholesome effect on the later development of the church, but in matters of doctrine and policy no concessions whatever were made. The Apocrypha were declared to be of equal authority with the Canonical Scriptures; church tradition was raised to a level with the Scriptures as a rule of faith and practise.

The Vulgate version of Jerome was made the official text of Scripture in all matters of interpretation. Justification was defined not as an act of God once for all whereby He imputes to the believer the perfect righteousness of Christ, appropriated by faith alone, but as a gradual infusion of righteousness in which process man may assist by good works.

The Sacrament of the Lord's Supper was declared to be a propitiatory sacrifice as well as a sacrament, and the bread and wine were regarded as converted into the essence of the body and blood of Christ. The cup was denied to the laity. The priesthood of the New Testament was declared to be a continuation of the priesthood of the Old Testament.

The doctrines regarding purgatory, worship of saints and relics, the efficacy of indulgences, the authority of the Pope, and others, were reaffirmed. The Council ended with pronouncement of, "Anathema to all heretics, Anathema, Anathema." The decrees of the Council were ratified by Pope Pius IV and the strict obedience to its decisions was enjoined on all Catholics. The Evangelicals had been consistently refused admission to the sessions of the Council and had no part in its deliberations and decisions.

Measures were shortly taken for the subjugation of all heretics by means of the terrible Inquisition which was set up in Spain, and which constitutes one of the darkest blots on the pages of the history of the church. The blood of the martyrs began to flow. Countless numbers were burnt at the stake. Others were thrown into filthy prison cells and subjected to unspeakable tortures in an effort to force them to renounce their faith.

Religious wars followed, notably the Thirty Years War, one of the most cruel and bloody wars of all history, pursued with the purpose of winning back for Rome the territories in Germany lost as a result of the Protestant Movement.

The decisive battle of this war was fought a century after the death of Luther, before Lützen, where the noble King Gustavus Adolphus of Sweden with thousands of his loyal subjects gave their lives that the fruits of the Reformation might be preserved for posterity.

The doctrines of the Roman Catholic Church were fixed for all time by the Council of Trent, but some notable additions have been made from time to time. Among these may be mentioned the doctrine of the Infallibility of the Pope as to all doctrinal decisions made ex cathedra, that is, in his official capacity as teacher of all Christians. This was promulgated by the Vatican Council in 1870.

The dogma regarding the Immaculate Conception of Mary was promulgated by Pope Pius IX (1846-48) which must be held by all believers on pain of excommunication and punishment. This doctrine, holding that Mary was untouched by all taint of original sin by birth, is the last link in the process of the deification of Mary begun by the Council at Ephesus A. D. 431, when Mary was declared the Mother of God. This virtually places Mary on the level with Jesus Christ, equally worthy with Him of Divine honor and worship.[36]

In 1928 was promulgated the notable encyclical Mortalium Animos which constitutes the Pope's answer to the Ecumenical Conferences held at Stockholm and Lausanne and also the Malines Conversations between representatives of the Church of England and the Church of Rome.

This famous encyclical presents "principles and reasons by which Catholics may know what to think and do in regard to those who strive to unite all those who bear the Christian name." The encyclical stresses the dogmas : Infallibility of the Pope; Value of the holy tradition as revelation from God; the power of the hierarchy; transubstantiation; worship of Mary the Mother of God; worship of images, and all the other features of the Romish system.[37]

This encyclical is sufficient indication of the present position of the Roman Catholic

Church as regards doctrine and as regards her attitude towards the churches of Protestantism. She regards all who are outside of Rome as lost sheep and she will welcome them back only on the condition of their accepting all the dogmas of the church and the overlordship of the Pope.

CHAPTER XI

Romanism and Lutheranism: A Striking Contrast.

Frequent references have already been made in the foregoing, as occasion has required, to the dogmas and practices of Romanism. However, nothing short of a systematic presentation of the tenets and principles of the Church of Rome in contrast with the tenets and principles of the Church of the Reformation will give an adequate conception of the wideness of the breach that exists between them.

Only the chief doctrines and concepts can be taken up for consideration and very briefly in each instance. For the sake of convenience the Roman and Lutheran teachings are grouped together under the various headings.

1. THE SCRIPTURES.

Rome claims: (a) The traditions of the Church are of equal value with Scripture as a Rule of Faith.

(b) The Scriptures can be interpreted only by an infallible Church of which the Pope is the head, who is infallible in all ex cathedra pronouncements on doctrines of faith and morals.

The Lutheran Church teaches: (a) The Scriptures are the sole Rule of Faith and Practice. (Matt. 15 : 3-6).

(b) The Church ought not to determine what Scripture teaches, but the Scriptures ought to fix the doctrines of the Church.

Every Christian has the privilege and the right to interpret Scripture by the guidance of the Holy Spirit and his own conscience. (Joh. 17 : 17; Acts 20 : 32).

2. JUSTIFICATION.

Roman Doctrine : According to the decrees of the Council of Trent, Justification is a gradual transition from a natural state to a state of grace in which man may assist by good works. In case it is lost by mortal sin and unbelief it may be regained by the sacrament of penance.[38]

Lutheran Doctrine : According to the Augsburg Confession, "men cannot be justified before God by their own strength, merits, or works, but are freely justified for Christ's sake thru faith". (Rom. 3: 23-24; Gal. 2. 16).

3. Sanctification.

According to the *Roman view*, Sanctification is achieved thru the various offices of the Church, including, unction, laying on of hands, mass, penance, absolution, good works, and the accumulated merits of the saints.

The *Lutheran Church* holds that Sanctification is a gift of God thru faith in Christ. Good works are performed as a fruit of the new life and not for the sake of merit. According to Luther: "Good works do not make a man good, but a good man will perform good works".

4. Indulgences.

According to the Catholic Catechism of Christian Doctrine: "The Church by means of Indulgences remits the temporal punishment due to sin by applying to us the merits of Jesus Christ, and the superabundant satisfactions of the Blessed Virgin Mary and of the saints; which merits and satisfactions are its spiritual treasury."[39]

The *Lutheran Church* teaches that the merits of Jesus Christ alone avail to satisfy the just demands of God, and that Christ alone is sufficient for all our needs. One believer cannot save another, for all are sinners in the sight of God. (Eph. 2 : 8-9; Heb. 4 : 16).

5. PURGATORY.

Rome: "Purgatory is the state in which those suffer for a time who die guilty of venial sins, or without having satisfied for the punishment due to their sins."

"The faithful on earth can help the souls in Purgatory by their prayers, fasts, almsdeeds; by indulgences, and by having Masses said for them." (Catechism of Christian Doctrine).[40]

The Lutheran Church: At death the spirit of the believer goes to the presence of Christ. Paul says to depart is to " be with Christ" which is "far better"; and Jesus says to the good and faithful servant, "well done"—"enter thou into the joy of thy Lord". (Phil. 1 : 23; Matt. 25 : 21).

6. Intermediaries.

Rome holds that the soul's approach to God must be mediated thru a host of intermediaries, Mary, departed saints, Pope, Cardinals, Bishops, Priests, and also thru Masses, Images, Pictures, etc.

In the book, "Glories of Mary" we read: "If my Redeemer rejects me on account of my sins, and drives me from his sacred feet, I will cast myself at those of his beloved Mother, till she has obtained my forgiveness." (p. 90).

"We often obtain more promptly what we ask by calling on the name of Mary than by invoking that of Jesus." (p. 112).

An inscription in Latin on a church near the Vatican reads: "Let us come boldly to the throne of the Virgin Mary that we may obtain grace to help in time of need".[41]

The Lutheran Church teaches, according to article twenty-one of the Augsburg Confession, that there is only one Mediator, Jesus Christ, our great high priest, our all sufficient sacrifice, and our intercessor before God, to whom prayer shall be made and homage given.

93

The saints shall be commemorated but not worshipped as for this there is no warrant in Scripture. (I Joh. 2 :1; I Tim. 2 :5).[42]

7. SUPREME AUTHORITY.

For *Rome* the seat of ultimate authority, up to 1870, was the Church and Church Councils, since then it is the Pope.

"These attributes (infallibility and indefectibility) are found in their fulness in the Pope, the visible head of the Church, whose infallible authority to teach bishops, priests, and people in matters of faith and morals will last to the end of world." (Catechism of Christian Doctrine).[43]

Lutherans teach that none is infallible except Christ himself and His Word of Truth delivered to us in the Scriptures. History shows that both popes and councils have erred and contradicted one another. Christ alone is the head of the church. (Col. 1 :18; Matt. 23 : 9-10).

8. THE SACRAMENTS.

Rome : "There are seven sacraments : Baptism, Confirmation, Holy Eucharist, Penance, Extreme Unction, Holy Orders, and

Matrimony." (Catechism of Christian Doctrine).[44]

According to the same source, "Baptism is a Sacrament which cleanses us from original sin, makes us Christians, children of God and heirs of heaven."

Regarding the Eucharist the Catholic Church teaches that the priest has the power to change the bread and wine into the substance of the body and blood of Christ. This doctrine is known as Transubstantiation. The cup is denied to the laity.

Lutherans recognize only two sacraments which were instituted by Christ himself. There is no Scripture warrant for other sacraments.

Baptism is held to be necessary according to the command of Christ. Therefore children should be baptized. God's grace is offered and given thru the act itself, but only those who receive it in faith will receive its blessings. (Mk. 16:16; Joh. 3:5, 18; Gal. 3:26; Tit. 3:5, 18).

In the Eucharist both elements, Christ's body and blood, are at hand and distributed to all who partake, under form of bread and wine. The participation in (koinonia) Christ's body and blood is held to be a spiritual and a sacramental participation and hence transcends every mere physical eating and drinking and every participation in and communion with Christ thru faith, prayer, or the reading and hearing of His Word. (Matt. 26 : 26-28; I Cor. 10 :16)).

The Sacrament of the Lord's Supper is received with blessing only by those who believe Christ's promise.[45]

9. EFFICACY OF THE SACRAMENTS.

Rome : The blessings and effects of the sacraments, as popularly conceived, follow automatically in fulfilling the act, irrespective of the state of heart of the recipient. This idea is conveyed by the phrase, "ex opere operato".[46]

Lutherans hold that the sacraments are valid from the point of view of God even if received unworthily, but they are of no value to the recipient unless received in faith. On the contrary, they are of positive harm. (I Cor. 11 : 27-29).

10. THE CHURCH.

Rome : "The Church is the congregation of all those who profess the faith of Christ, partake of the same sacraments, and are governed by their lawful pastors under one visible head." (Catechism of Christian Doctrine).[47]

The church is regarded as in itself a medium of salvation.

The *Lutheran Church* teaches that the Church is the congregation of saints, in which the Gospel is rightly taught and the sacraments rightly administered. It is conceived of as a medium of salvation only in so far as it preaches Christ.

The Kingdom of God is not infallibly present where the external church is found, but wherever Christ is preached there is Christ's kingdom and the church in the ideal sense. (Eph. 2: 19-22; 4: 4-5; I Cor. 12: 13).[48]

CHAPTER XII

The Church of Rome: Its Basic Claims.

Not only is the Roman Catholic Church far removed from the Lutheran Church as to its fundamental doctrines, but it is diametrically opposed to all evangelical conceptions as to its basic claims and its fundamental nature and cultus.   It has absorbed so many extraneous elements thruout the course of its history that it is far removed from Apostolic Christianity and can scarcely any longer be recognized as the church founded by Jesus Christ.

Let us examine first of all the Roman claims as to the *unity and power of the church.*   The Bull Unam Sanctam promulgated by Pope Boniface in 1302 begins: "One holy, catholic, and apostolic church, we are compelled by faith to admit and to hold." The proofs adduced as to the unity of the church are by no means convincing, as for instance: In Noah's time there was only one ark for the salvation of the world; therefore there can be only one church; Christ's garment was one and indivisible; Christ says to Peter, "Feed my sheep"; the "my" here is inclusive, all are included.[49]

As to the power of the church, it is conceived of under two aspects, the temporal and the spiritual; these are spoken of as the two swords. The Scripture proof for this assumption is discovered in the words of Peter : "Lord, here are two swords", and Jesus answers, "It is enough". (Luke 22: 38). The Bull goes on to elaborate the doctrine of the two swords. One temporal shall be carried *for* the church, one spiritual shall be carried *by* the church. But the temporal shall be subject to the spiritual. (According to Rom. 13: 1). As a matter of fact this passage of Scripture teaches the direct opposite of this Roman assumption. Paul says here : "Let every soul (and this includes the Pope and the Roman Curia) be in subjection to the higher powers : for there is no power but of God; and the powers that be are ordained of God". From the context it is clear that Paul is speaking of the temporal rulers whom he designates by the term, "higher powers".

As to the ultimate seat of authority, the Bull has this to offer: "Therefore we declare, promulgate, and determine that it is necessary to salvation for every created human being to subordinate himself under the authority of the Pope at Rome."

With these high pretensions compare the words of Jesus to His disciples: "Whosoever would be first among you, shall be servant of all", and, "I am in the midst of you as he that serveth". (Mk. 10 : 44; Luke 22 : 27). In viewing this contrast one is not surprised to learn that Luther regarded the Pope as antichrist.

Now as to the manifest teaching of Scripture regarding the temporal and spiritual powers, these are distinct and separate and should not be mixed or confounded. Jesus says: "My kingdom is not of this world"; and Paul avers, "The weapons of our warfare are not of the flesh". (Joh. 18 :36; II Cor. 10 :4).

The spiritual power shall not interfere with the temporal power nor annul the same.

"Render therefore unto Caesar the things that are Caesar's; and unto God the things that are God's". (Matt. 22:21).

The power of the keys, that is, churchly authority, extends to the preaching of the Gospel, the forgiveness and withholding of forgiveness of sins, and the dispensing of the sacraments. (Matt. 28: 19-20; Joh. 20: 21-23).

According to Luther the functions of the church are two: The church is a missionary institution, and a school for those who are not yet true Christians. Therefore the church is neither competent nor authorized to permanently lead, rule, or hold in tutelage the true Christians. All Christians are priests and able and competent to decide for themselves on questions of religious and moral life. (I Pet. 2:5. 9; Joh. 16 :).[50] These principles laid down by Luther sound rather strange in the ears of the church-centered Lutheranism of our day.

CHAPTER XIII

The Church of Rome: Its Fundamental Nature and Cultus.

Let us now examine the Church of Rome as to its *fundamental nature and cultus.* In this matter we are fortunate in having inside expert information from one who has for many years himself been a devout Catholic, but later embraced evangelical principles and went over to the Protestant faith.

Friedrich Heiler, in his book Catholicism, maintains as his earnest conviction that the Roman Catholic Church as now constituted is not the organ of salvation founded by the historical Christ.

He demonstrates convincingly and in some detail that Catholicism is composed of five distinct constituent elements :

(1) The primitive popular cults—Paganism;

(2) The strict legalistic religion—Judaism;

(3) The hierarchical ruler-religion—Romanism;

(4) The mystical salvation cults—Hellenism; and,

(5) The Biblical-evangelical revelation—The Gospel.

The five elements may be further summed up under three heads : Heathendom, Judaism, and Christianity. Catholicism may thus be characterized as a great syncretism, a huge complex of various heterogeneous elements so mixed and blended as to form one compact unified system.[51]

As examples of the heathen cult influence may be mentioned the superstition, magic, and credulity so prevalent in the Roman Catholic Church. It is essentially a ritualistic and sacramental religion. There is a magic power in the rites themselves, the holy articles themselves, to bring blessings to those who use them or for whom they are used.

The priest is a miracle worker. In the Eucharist the priest compels God to come down and assume corporeal form, and God obeys. Karl Barth enlarges upon the enviable role of the priest before the altar as he elevates the elements and thus becomes a Creator Creatoris before the people, and also is not essentially evangelical, but is rather related to the heathen mystical cults.

The hierarchical system which holds the entire Catholic world in its mighty grip has been pictured in its workings in the foregoing pages and there is no need to enlarge upon it here. This hierarchical system is a direct descendant of the Roman genius for government, law, and rule. It is the old passion of Rome for world domination and rule, perpetuated within the church.

Finally there is the true salvation by grace, the evangelical ingredient, which must not be forgotten. How it lives on in this vast syncretistic system is a mystery to many, but the fact is that it does, tho it does not occupy a central place and is often crowded into the background.[54]

Nowhere else do the distinctive differences between the Catholic and Evangelical viewpoints appear so strikingly as in the conception of faith.

Faith, from the Evangelical viewpoint is in Christ and his finished work; from the Catholic viewpoint it is in the church, its doctrines and means of salvation. Faith is itself looked upon as an act of obedience and therefore carries merit, it is not a gift of the grace of God. Faith therefore in its practical aspects amounts to submission to the authority of the church and obedience to its laws.

Archbishop Söderblom has characterized this kind of faith as "quantitative", in contrast with the simple saving and life giving faith in Christ Jesus on the part of the Evangelical Christian. According to the Roman Catholic view it is necessary to salvation not only to accept Jesus Christ as Savior, but also it is of equal importance to accept the dogmas of the Church regarding the infallibility of the Pope, transubstantiation, the worship of Mary as Mother of God, the immaculate conception, and a host of others.[55]

CHAPTER XIV

CONCLUSION

Enough has been said to demonstrate the wideness of the gulf that exists between the Roman Catholic Church and the churches of Evangelical Christianity, particularly the Lutheran Church.

Because of these fundamental differences in doctrine and viewpoint as well as practice, aside from the question of attitude, there is small hope of any union between Catholic and Evangelical Christianity, even were such a union desirable.

As Lutherans we deplore as much as any the breach in the Church of Christ. We have seen how Luther and his followers were loth to bring about the break with Rome, and how ready they were to adopt a conciliatory attitude towards Rome, in the hopes of healing the breach after it had already been made.

Yet they were not willing, nor should we be willing, to give up dearly bot spiritual privileges for the sake of mere outward uniformity in organization and practice, and the advantages gained thereby.

As we study the development and the dogmatic fixing and standardization of error as it has taken place in the Church of Rome we realize more fully the truth of the statement by one servant of God to the effect that error once admitted into the church is never wholly eradicated, but lives on and tends to become more aggravated as time goes on.

May the Lutheran Church in the future as in the past always be characterized by a genuine zeal for the truth and for the pure Gospel as delivered to us by Christ and His disciples.

The pure Gospel and the advantages gained for us by Luther and the other reformers may be lost to us in one of two ways : either by capitulation to the enemies of the Gospel, which God forbid may ever come to pass; or by capitulation to our own indolence and lack of desire for a vigorous use of our spiritual faculties.

We may not be called upon to face the eventuality of being burned alive at the stake as Luther and many of his associates faced that danger; but we do stand in the even greater danger of having our spiritual life smothered by the weeds of sloth and the thorns of unholy desire.

"Hold fast that which thou hast, that no one take thy crown".

Holding fast, however, does not imply standing still. In a time of looseness of confession on the one hand, and of fossilized rigidity of doctrine on the other, we need to hold fast what we have. Yet, on the basis of what has been gained in the past, we need to advance to a greater realization of God's truth, and a greater enjoyment of our God-given heritage.

Our confessions are but mile-posts along the way, marking the places of hard fought battles and dearly bot victories; they are not terminals where ends our endeavour and our quest for spiritual treasure. Our confessions should be a means and a challenge to us to advance on the road of spiritual knowledge and discernment and to sink ourselves yet deeper into the mine of God's truth. In this the Reformers themselves are our example and our inspiration.

LUTHER'S BREAK WITH ROME

Lord, keep us steadfast in Thy Word;
Curb those who fain by craft or sword
Would wrest the kingdom from Thy Son,
And set at naught all He hath done.

Lord Jesus Christ, Thy power make known,
For Thou art Lord of lords alone;
Defend Thy Christendom, that we
May evermore sing praise to Thee.

Martin Luther, 1541.

REFERENCES

The following is a list of the most important references consulted in the preparation of this book:

1. Luther in the Light of Recent Research. Heinrich Böhmer. Christian Herald Pub. Co., New York, 1916. 323 pp.

2. Katolicismen. Friedrich Heiler. Översatt av Ingrid Ljungquist. Stockholm, Sv. Kristliga Studentrörelsens förl., 1920. 168 pp.

3. Kirkehistoriske Läsestycker. Helge Haar og Jens Nörregaard. Köbenhavn. Vol. I, 1914, 128 pp; Vol. II, 1916, 179 pp.

4. Luther and the Reformation. James Mackinnon. Longmans, Green, and Co., London. Vol. I, 1925, 317 pp; Vol. II, 1928, 354 pp; Vol. III, 1929, 338 pp; Vol. IV, 1930, 372 pp.

REFERENCES

5. History of the Christian Church. Philip Schaff. Vol. VI, 1916. Scribners, New York. 755 pp.

6. Church History. Kurz. Vol. II. Funk & Wagnalls Co., New York, 1889. 478 pp.

7. The Confessional History of the Lutheran Church. James W. Richard. Lutheran Pub. Soc., Philadelphia, 1909. 637 pp.

8. The Making and Meaning of the Augsburg Confession. Conrad Bergendoff. Augustana Book Concern, Rock Island, Ill., 1930. 127 pp.

9. Dr. Martin Luther's Deutsche Schriften. Ernest Ludwig Enders. Erlangen Ed., 1885. 67 vols.

10. Dokumente zum Ablasstreit von 1517. W. Köhler. Mohr, Tübingen und Leipzig, 1902. 160 pp.

11. Augsburgiska Bekännelsen. N. Forsander. Augustana Book Concern, Rock Island, Ill., 1902. 124 pp.

12. A Catechism of Christian Doctrine. Prepared and Enjoined by the Third Plenary Council of Baltimore. Published

REFERENCES

by Ecclesiastical Authority. Kilner & Co., Philadelphia, 1920. No. 2. 64 pp.

13. The Word of God and the Word of Man. Karl Barth. Pilgrim Press, 1928. 327 pp.

14. Påvestolen och Kyrkans Enhet. Nathan Söderblom. Augustana Quarterly, Rock Island, Ill., June, 1928. p 97 ff.

15. Why We Are Protestants. W. Graham Scroggie. The Evangelical Quarterly, Edinburg, October, 1929. p 367 ff.

16. The "Miracles" at Malden. Literary Digest, New York, December 7, 1929. p 22 f.

17. International Standard Bible Encyclopedia. Chicago, 1915.

18. Encyclopedia Brittanica. New York, 14th Ed. 1930.

REFERENCES IN THE TEXT

[1] Böhmer p 123 ff
[2] Köhler p 37
[3] Böhmer p 128
[4] Mackinnon Vol. I, p 291
[5] Köhler p 125 (Author's translation)
[6] Enders Vol. 26, p 19 ff
[7] Mackinnon Vol. I, p 296
[8] Köhler p 127 ff (Author's translation)
[9] Böhmer p 134 ff
[10] Mackinnon Vol. II, p 37 ff
[11] Kurz p 234
[12] Mackinnon Vol. II, p 81 ff
[13] Mackinnon Vol. II, p 144 f
[14] Schaff Vol. VI, p 207 ff
[15] Schaff Vol. VI, p 213 ff
[16] Schaff Vol. VI, p 220 ff; Mackinnon Vol. II, p 263 ff
[17] Haar og Nörregaard Vol. II, p 26 ff
[18] Schaff Vol. VI, p 225
[19] Haar og Nörregaard Vol. II, p 26
[20] Schaff Vol. VI, p 248; Mackinnon Vol. II, p 213

[21]Mackinnon Vol. II, p 192 ff

[22]Mackinnon Vol. II, p 290; Schaff Vol. VI, p 300 ff

[23]Schaff Vol. VI, p 330 ff; Mackinnon Vol. III, p 1 ff

[24]Böhmer p 148 ff

[25]Schaff Vol. VI, p 690 ff

[26]Schaff Vol. VI, p 276, 696 ff; Richard p 24 ff

[27]Mackinnon Vol. IV, p 1 ff; Richard p 54

[28]Richard p 61 ff

[29]Richard p 194 ff

[30]Schaff Vol. VI, p 698 ff

[31]Richard p 99 ff; Bergendoff p 33 ff

[32]Richard p 97 ff

[33]Mackinnon Vol. IV, p 7 ff

[34]Richard p 192 f

[35]Int. St. Bible Enc. Article: Council of Trent; Kurz p 293 ff

[36]Heiler p 35 ff; Int. St. Bible Enc. Various articles

[37]Söderblom p 97 ff

[38]Int. St. Bible Enc. Article: Council of Trent

[39]Catechism of Chr. Doct. p 36

[40]Catechism of Chr. Doct. p 63

[41]Scroggie p 376

References in the Text

[42]Bergendoff p 89
[43]Catechism of Chr. Doct. p 20
[44]Catechism of Chr. Doct. p 22
[45]Forsander p 90
[46]Heiler p 25
[47]Catechism of Chr. Doct. p 19 ff
[48]Forsander p 77 ff; Böhmer p 294
[49]Haag og Nörregaard Vol. I, p 110 f
[50]Böhmer p 295
[51]Heiler p 22 ff
[52]Barth p 113
[53]Digest p 22
[54]Heiler p 73 ff
[55]Söderblom p 97 ff